SPOTLIGHT ON A FAIR AND EQUAL SOCIETY

SOCIAL JUSTICE THROUGH ACTIVISM

DANIELLE HAYNES

PowerKiDS press

Published in 2023 by The Rosen Publishing Group, Inc.
2544 Clinton St, Buffalo, NY 14224

Copyright © 2023 by The Rosen Publishing Group, Inc.

All rights reserved. No part of this book may be reproduced in any form without permission in writing from the publisher, except by a reviewer.

First Edition

Editor: Greg Roza
Book Design: Michael Flynn

Photo Credits: Cover Ermolaev Alexander/Shutterstock.com; (series background) tavizta/Shutterstock.com; p. 5 CarlosBarquero/Shutterstock.com; p. 6 StunningArt/Shutterstock.com; p. 7 iam2mai/Shutterstock.com; p. 9 https://en.wikipedia.org/wiki/Amariyanna_Copeny#/media/File:Barack_Obama_hugs_Mari_Copeny.jpg; p. 10 https://commons.wikimedia.org/wiki/File:Ludington_statue_800.jpg; p. 11 courtesy of the Library of Congress; p. 13 Will Counts/Arkansas Democrat-Gazette/AP Images; p. 14 fizkes/Shutterstock.com; p. 15 https://commons.wikimedia.org/wiki/File:Housing_in_a_Japanese_Relocation_camp_-_NARA_-_195540.jpg; p. 17 dominika zara/Shutterstock.com; p. 19 S-F/Shutterstock.com; p. 21 Ben Birchall/PA Wire/AP Images; p. 22 Cavan-Images/Shutterstock.com; p. 23 Antonio Guillem/Shutterstock.com; p. 25 Kathy Hutchins/Shutterstock.com; p. 27 Jordan Strauss/Invision/AP Images; p. 29 Daisy Daisy/Shutterstock.com; p. 30 elenabsl/Shutterstock.com.

Library of Congress Cataloging-in-Publication Data

Names: Haynes, Danielle, author.
Title: Social justice through activism / Danielle Haynes.
Description: Buffalo, NY : PowerKids Press, [2023] | Series: Spotlight on a fair and equal society | Includes index.
Identifiers: LCCN 2021055195 (print) | LCCN 2021055196 (ebook) | ISBN 9781538387832 (library binding) | ISBN 9781538387801 (paperback) | ISBN 9781538387849 (ebook)
Subjects: LCSH: Youth--Political activity--Juvenile literature. | Teenagers--Political activity--Juvenile literature. | Social justice--Juvenile literature. | Political activism--Juvenile literature.
Classification: LCC HQ799.2.P6 H387 2023 (print) | LCC HQ799.2.P6 (ebook) | DDC 305.235--dc23/eng/20220224
LC record available at https://lccn.loc.gov/2021055195
LC ebook record available at https://lccn.loc.gov/2021055196

Manufactured in the United States of America

Some of the images in this book illustrate individuals who are models. The depictions do not imply actual situations or events.

CPSIA Compliance Information: Batch #CWPK23. For further information contact Rosen Publishing, New York, New York at 1-800-237-9932.

CONTENTS

- ACTIVISM IN OUR WORLD 4
- WHAT ARE INEQUALITY AND INEQUITY? 6
- A PATH TO SOCIAL JUSTICE 8
- YOUTH AS ACTIVE CITIZENS 10
- WHO WERE THE LITTLE ROCK NINE? 12
- HOW CAN EMPATHY HELP? 14
- WHAT IS SOCIAL RESPONSIBILITY? 16
- YOU CAN HELP! 18
- AN INSPIRING YOUTH ACTIVIST 20
- SKILL SET FOR ACTIVE CITIZENS 22
- REACHING OUT 24
- STANDING UP FOR YOUR RIGHTS 26
- TIME TO ACT 28
- GLOSSARY 31
- INDEX 32
- PRIMARY SOURCE LIST 32

CHAPTER ONE

ACTIVISM IN OUR WORLD

We live in a world full of different **cultures** and experiences. People may have different skin tones, experience gender in various ways, or speak a different language. This makes the world a rich and interesting place to live. But it can also lead to problems with equality and equity. We can make a choice to be part of the solutions.

A classmate who lives in a different neighborhood from you may not have the same clean water you do. Maybe your religion or the color of your skin means you face unfair treatment at school. When you step up or speak up to respond to these injustices, you're part of the solution.

Being an active citizen can make a difference in big or small ways. Activism helps educate others and create positive change in the world.

> You can make a choice to be a part of the problem or a part of the solution.

CHAPTER TWO

WHAT ARE INEQUALITY AND INEQUITY?

"Inequality" deals with size in numbers. For example, pay inequality is a term for how people who do the same work are paid differently. "Inequity" means a lack of fairness or justice.

> Equality doesn't always mean everyone has the same chance at success.

EQUALITY VS. EQUITY

Imagine a family of three—two adults and one child. Equality means you give each of them the same size box to stand on in order to see over a tall fence. The box might be too short for the child and just right for one of the adults. It might not be needed at all for the tallest adult.

Equity means you give each of the family members something different to suit their needs. So, the child will get two boxes, the shorter adult will get one box, and the tallest adult won't get any boxes at all.

CHAPTER THREE
A PATH TO SOCIAL JUSTICE

Active and responsible citizens deal with both inequality and inequity. They call attention to an issue or injustice. This might be climate change, the rights of the disabled, or **discrimination**. Activism helps with social justice. Social justice is the view that everyone deserves equal rights.

Take Mari Copeny (aka Little Miss Flint), for instance. In 2014, the people of the city of Flint, Michigan, started getting sick from drinking the city's water. The government had recently switched water sources. Because of poor treatment and testing, this water was full of lead. The Flint water crisis mostly affected people of color and those in poorer neighborhoods.

Many activists stepped up, including Mari. When she was 8 years old, she wrote a letter to President Barack Obama about the problem. He later visited the city and made sure it received $100 million to help with the water issues.

Mari Copeny inspired President Barack Obama to visit the city of Flint to talk to leaders and residents about how the water crisis affected the community.

CHAPTER FOUR

YOUTH AS ACTIVE CITIZENS

Young people have often been active citizens. Some took part in the U.S. fight for independence from Great Britain. At age 16, in 1777, Sybil Ludington rode a horse over 40 miles (64.4 km) to warn people in New York about an attack by the British. In the next century, a teenager from Philadelphia, Pennsylvania, named Anna Elizabeth Dickinson became an activist when she started writing and speaking publicly against slavery.

Even though Sybil Ludington rode farther than Paul Revere and her task was just as important, Revere is more well known because of a famous poem by Henry Wadsworth Longfellow.

ANNA ELIZABETH DICKINSON

Young Americans were actively a part of the fight for civil rights in the 1950s and 1960s. During this time, U.S. schools were largely **segregated**. This meant that white students went to certain schools, while Black students went to others. The 1954 Supreme Court decision *Brown v. Board of Education* said racially segregated schools were **unconstitutional**. The decision was supposed to officially end segregation, but many schools refused to stop segregating classrooms.

CHAPTER FIVE
WHO WERE THE LITTLE ROCK NINE?

In September 1957, the fight over desegregation boiled over in Little Rock, Arkansas. Civil rights leaders wanted to force the state to integrate, so they chose nine brave Black students to register at Central High School. These students came to be known as the Little Rock Nine. Their names were Minnijean Brown, Elizabeth Eckford, Ernest Green, Thelma Mothershed, Melba Patillo, Gloria Ray, Terrence Roberts, Jefferson Thomas, and Carlotta Walls.

President Dwight D. Eisenhower ordered troops to walk with the students into school. All nine students were supposed to enter the school together. But Elizabeth arrived alone. A photograph of her walking on the school grounds by herself, surrounded by students and adults yelling at her, has become one of the most well-known images of the civil rights struggle.

Elizabeth Eckford arrived at Central High School alone for the first day of classes and was met with screaming and insults. She was even spat upon.

CHAPTER SIX

HOW CAN EMPATHY HELP?

Empathy is understanding and sharing other people's thoughts, emotions, or experiences. Having empathy toward others helps us think about how our own actions may affect others. A first step to empathy is awareness of injustice.

Few people spoke out against the Japanese American internment camps. This is why we need to encourage empathy. Having empathy can make people want to act.

When the United States was at war with Japan as part of World War II in the 1940s, the government forced about 120,000 Japanese American citizens to leave their homes. They were moved to large camps where they were forced to live without freedom or respect because of their **ethnicity**. A number of people have written about conditions in the camps. One of them is an actor named George Takei. He was one of the many children in the camps. Takei has worked to raise awareness of this injustice. When we read about other people's experiences, we often learn and experience empathy toward them.

CHAPTER SEVEN
WHAT IS SOCIAL RESPONSIBILITY?

Social responsibility is the idea that people are expected to take actions that benefit all of society. Some people, organizations, or governments act solely for the good of the few or for those in power instead of the good of all. It's up to everyone else to recognize such unfairness and speak up.

Pay attention to groups that could be treated unfairly or with **prejudice**. These groups might include women, racial minorities, people with disabilities, or people who live in poor neighborhoods. You probably know many **marginalized** people like this and might be part of these groups yourself.

It's up to all of us, whether we belong to one of those groups or not, to listen to marginalized voices and support them. The hope is that you can bring about real change in the world.

The Special Olympics is the world's largest sports organization for people with intellectual and physical disabilities. Special Olympics athletes have a special oath: "Let me win, but if I cannot win, let me be brave in the attempt."

CHAPTER EIGHT

YOU CAN HELP!

Acts of activism can be big or small depending on the problem and what you're comfortable doing about it. Here are some ideas:

USE YOUR VOICE
Sometimes the easiest thing to do is simply to say something. If you see a classmate getting bullied because of their religion or another reason, tell the bully to stop or get an adult involved.

WRITE
Sometimes you might want to reach more people. Do you want to draw attention to a problem in your community? Write a letter to your local newspaper or community leaders.

ORGANIZE
Join or organize a school group. There are all kinds of groups actively working for change and social justice.

Standing up for what you believe is right is the basis for becoming an active citizen.

PROTEST

Perhaps one of the most widely known forms of activism is **protesting**. Protests can include just a handful of people or millions calling attention to injustice.

CHAPTER NINE
AN INSPIRING YOUTH ACTIVIST

It may seem hard to believe that young people can have a big impact on the world. But think about Malala Yousafzai. At about 11 years old, she wrote online about what it was like living under Taliban rule in Pakistan. This religious group wanted to take over the government and stop girls from going to school, among other things.

In 2012, the Taliban shot Malala when she was just 15 years old. They tried—and failed—to kill her because she spoke out publicly on girls' right to an education. After healing, she started the Malala Fund, which raises and donates money to this cause. In 2014, at just 17 years old, Malala became the youngest person to win a Nobel Peace Prize.

Malala Yousafzai won the Nobel Peace Prize in 2014 for **advocating** for girls' education.

CHAPTER TEN

SKILL SET FOR ACTIVE CITIZENS

Active citizens need a certain skill set. These skills are different depending on what type of activism you want to take part in.

Good **communication** skills are important for almost any type of group effort. Think about it—activism is all about communicating information to a small or large group of people. This happens both in writing and in speech. Even posters and banners are a type of communication.

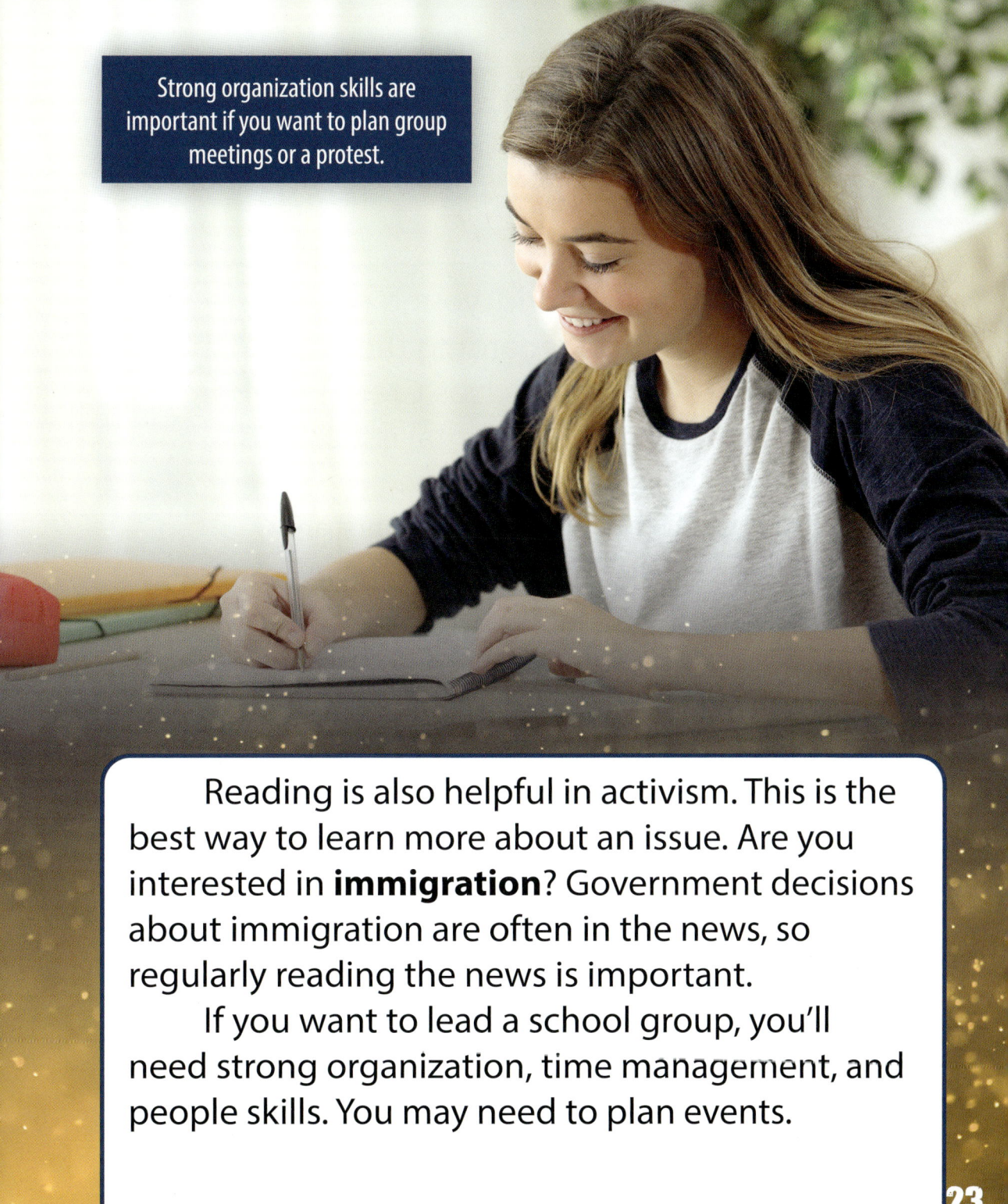

Strong organization skills are important if you want to plan group meetings or a protest.

Reading is also helpful in activism. This is the best way to learn more about an issue. Are you interested in **immigration**? Government decisions about immigration are often in the news, so regularly reading the news is important.

If you want to lead a school group, you'll need strong organization, time management, and people skills. You may need to plan events.

CHAPTER ELEVEN

REACHING OUT

Throughout the world, young people are becoming more vocal regarding the state of the **environment**. Activists such as Greta Thunberg draw attention to environmental issues and inspire others to get involved.

Xiuhtezcatl (shoo-TEZ-kawt) Martinez—sometimes just called X—is an American youth activist and hip-hop artist. He speaks out about environmental issues as well as problems faced by **indigenous** peoples of North America. When he was just 6, Martinez made his first speech to a crowd of adults. He stressed the importance of teaching the world's youth to protect the natural world.

Martinez has continued to be a strong voice in environmental activism. He asserts that a sense of community can help us come together to make positive changes. Reaching out to others in the community is an important step when it comes to activism.

Martinez believes that, "The most important work that can be done to **steward** our planet is to strengthen our relationship with our communities. Whether it is a climate crisis or a global pandemic, we need each other."

CHAPTER TWELVE
STANDING UP FOR YOUR RIGHTS

At its heart, injustice means a person or a system with power is using it unjustly. Whether it's a bully who's bigger than you, a government, or a system, it can be scary to go against it.

But that's what Loretta Claiborne did.

Claiborne was born with several physical and intellectual disabilities. She's partially blind, and she didn't walk or talk until she was 4 years old. She was bullied in school and became very angry about this as a teenager.

When she was 17, Claiborne's school counselor suggested that she compete in the newly formed Special Olympics. Over the course of six Special Olympics, Claiborne won four gold medals in running! She has gone on to many other achievements in the world of sports.

Claiborne has used her success to change the way people view individuals with disabilities. She has become a well-respected activist.

Claiborne is a true inspiration to people of all abilities. She speaks five languages, has a black belt in karate, and was honored with the Arthur Ashe Courage Award. She is also a member of the Special Olympics International Board of Directors.

CHAPTER THIRTEEN

TIME TO ACT

How do you know the best way to take action? There are so many important causes. Say, for instance, that people who use wheelchairs can't attend field trips at your school. The school doesn't use accessible buses for such trips.

You think it's unfair that some people can't go even though they want to. What should you do? If you don't use a wheelchair, the best way to start is to talk to the students affected. Help to support their work to fix the problem instead of trying to take over.

If you do use a wheelchair, think about what you can do to speak up and advocate for yourself and others. Talk to an adult at school. Check to see if there's a disability rights group on campus you could join.

What if simply asking for change doesn't work? At some point, parents and teachers might need to help you bring the issue to school leaders. They'll be able to draw from their own experience to guide you. It might also draw the attention of local news teams and reporters, who might then draw more attention to your cause.

If all else fails, bigger advocacy groups with lots of resources—such as the American Civil Liberties Union—might be able to help sue the school for equal treatment of all students. Activism is important to living in a society, whether it takes place in the classroom or in the streets. By working to help, you'll learn empathy for those around you and hopefully make a big change in the world.

GLOSSARY

advocate (ADD-vuh-kayt) To support or argue for a cause.

communication (kuh-myoo-nuh-KAY-shun) The use of words, sounds, signs, or behaviors to convey ideas, thoughts, and feelings.

culture (KUHL-chuhr) The beliefs and ways of life of a certain group of people.

discrimination (dih-scrih-muh-NAY-shun) Different—usually unfair—treatment based on factors such as a person's race, age, religion, or gender.

environment (ihn-VIY-ruhn-muht) The natural world around us.

ethnicity (eth-NIH-sih-tee) The quality of belonging to a group made up of people who share a common cultural background.

immigration (ih-muh-GRAY-shun) The act of coming to a country to settle there.

indigenous (in-DIH-jeh-ness) Related to the earliest known inhabitants of a place.

marginalized (MAR-juh-nuh-lyzd) Related to a position on the outside of a group or society.

prejudice (PREH-juh-duhs) An unfair feeling of dislike for a person or group because of race or religious or other beliefs.

protest (PRO-test) To show disagreement with something, sometimes at a public event.

segregate (SEH-gruh-gayt) To separate people based on race, class, or ethnicity.

steward (STOO-wurd) To manage and protect something, such as the environment and planet.

unconstitutional (un-kahn-stuh-TOO-shuh-nuhl) Not legal under a constitution.

INDEX

A
American Civil Liberties Union, 30

B
Brown, Minnijean, 12
Brown v. Board of Education, 11

C
Claiborne, Loretta, 26, 27
Copeny, Mari, 8, 9

D
Dickinson, Anna Elizabeth, 10, 11

E
Eckford, Elizabeth, 12, 13
Eisenhower, Dwight, 12

F
Flint water crisis, 8, 9

G
Great Britain, 10
Green, Ernest, 12

J
Japanese American internment camps, 15

L
Little Rock Nine, 12, 13
Luddington, Sybil, 10

M
Martinez (X), Xiuhtezcatl, 24, 25
Mothershed, Thelma, 12

O
Obama, Barack, 8, 9

P
Patillo, Melba, 12

R
Ray, Gloria, 12
Revere, Paul, 10
Roberts, Terrance, 12

S
segregation, 11, 12, 13
Special Olympics, 17, 26, 27
Supreme Court, 11

T
Takei, George, 15
Thomas, Jefferson, 12
Thunberg, Greta, 24

W
Walls, Carlotta, 12
World War II, 15

Y
Yousafzai, Malala, 20, 21

PRIMARY SOURCE LIST

Page 13
Elizabeth Eckford arriving at Central High School as white classmates jeer. Photograph. 1957. Little Rock, Arkansas. Held by the Bettman collection.

Page 19
People take part in the Global Strike for Climate. Photograph. September 27, 2019. Toronto, Ontario, Canada. Held by Shutterstock.

Page 21
Malala Yousafzai. Photograph. October 10, 2014. Birmingham, England. Held by AFP.